PRAY...
HIGHLAN...

Uniform with this volume

PRAYING WITH SAINT FRANCIS
PRAYING WITH SAINT AUGUSTINE
PRAYING WITH THE NEW TESTAMENT

Other titles in preparation

PRAYING WITH
Highland Christians

A selection from
POEMS OF THE WESTERN HIGHLANDERS
by G. R. D. McLean

Foreword by Sally Magnusson

TRI△NGLE

First published 1988
Triangle
SPCK
Holy Trinity Church
Marylebone Road
London NW1 4DU

British Library Cataloguing in Publication Data

Carmichael, Alexander
  [Carmina Gadelica. *English. Selections*]
  Praying with Highland Christians: a selection from
  Poems of the Western Highlanders.—(Praying with . . .).
  1. Prayer-books
  I. Title   II. McLean, G. R. D.   III. Series
  242'.8   BV245

  ISBN 0-281-04342-6

Typeset by Rowland Phototypesetting Ltd
Bury St Edmunds, Suffolk
Reproduced, printed and bound in Great Britain by
Hazell Watson & Viney Limited
Member of BPCC plc
Aylesbury Bucks

Contents

Foreword
by Sally Magnusson

My command of the Gaelic language is, let's face it, limited. As a matter of fact, it consists solely of being able to impart to any passing Gael the information that 'there are four trees on the island', this being the only practical legacy of a happy fortnight's Gaelic-learning on the Isle of Skye some years ago. Naturally this botanical revelation doesn't get me very far in the Hebrides and I've no idea why that one phrase (*tha ceithir craobhan air an eilean*) has clung so tenaciously to my memory when everything else had departed long before I got off the ferry.

But what I have retained from that time, rather less tangibly, is a sense of awe at the richness of the language and the ancient culture of Gaeldom, mingled with a piercing shame at how ill-equipped I, as a lowland Scot, am to appreciate them. And that is one reason why this volume of old, old Gaelic prayers, so lovingly translated by the late G. R. D. McLean, is such a delight. It opens up a world about which I knew next to nothing and it does so with a freshness that simply compels me to inhabit it.

We live with the writers of these prayers through the darkness of their long, dangerous nights, as they ask blessing upon their fires and peats and protection from the raging ocean, as they beg that sin may flee like 'the mist of the morning on the crest of the hills' and praise God the great chieftain of the clan of men. It is a fascinating glimpse into the lives and preoccupations of these people.

The great surprise, though, is how utterly familiar they turn out to be. That again is why I turn the pages of this collection with such relish. Their prayers are the eternal cries of the believer to his God: cries of joy and pain and fear and contrition, sighs of hope and longing, pleas for blessings and forgiveness, robust paeans of praise and thankfulness. Whether you're a stock-broker in Surrey or a crofter on Lewis, there are sentiments and a quality of emotion in these simple, repetitive refrains which every Christian must know.

> As from my mouth my prayer upriseth clear,
> May I feel in my heart that thou art here,

pleads one writer, expressing for everyone the time-less longing of the human spirit that we may know our prayers are heard. And whether you sleep in a man-sion or a high-rise flat, a semi or a bungalow, or indeed the sort of hovel that this writer probably dwelt in, here is a night-blessing that speaks for us all:

> The dwelling, O God, by thee be blest,
> And each one who here this night doth rest;
> My dear ones, O God, bless thou and keep
> In every place where they are asleep;
>
> In the evening that doth fall tonight,
> And in every single evening-light;
> In the daylight that doth make today,
> And in every single daylight-ray.

Lovely prayers of the evening like that one made a particular impression on me, perhaps because we all crave protection and blessing in the night, we all wish our home secure and our children safe from harm, and every believer longs to feel his God close as the night draws in. I have rarely seen it put more eloquently than by these anonymous Celtic Christians, as they review the experiences of the day and look forward to a night under God's shield, drawing on the resources of their art to express the intimacies of their faith.

Their prayers invite us to speak them aloud: the vocabulary is simple and the translator's rhymes are easy; often the same thought is repeated over and over, almost like a chant. But the rhyming and the repetitiveness also bestow a formal gravity that in-hibits glibness:

O God of life, this night
O darken not to me thy light,
O God of life, this night
Close not thy gladness to my sight,
O God of Life, this night
Thy door to me o shut not tight,
O God of life, this night
Refuse not mercy to my plight,
O God of life, this night
Quell unto me thy grieving slight,
O God of life, this night
Crown thou to me thy joy's delight,
O crown to me thy joy's delight,
O God of life, this night.

Perhaps the reason I love that one so much is that it simply says everything so much better than I could. It is a privilege to pray with these Celtic Christians. Their conversations with the God they loved all those years ago must surely enhance our own, just as their humanity and their faith can only enlarge ours.

Sally Magnusson

Publisher's Note

The prayers in this book are translations of traditional Gaelic poems selected from the Reverend G. R. D. McLean's *Poems of the Western Highlanders*, first published by SPCK in 1961. The genesis of that volume was described by McLean in his Introduction, as follows:

This work is the result of some ten years or so of labour and study. A chance meeting and a chance word in Inverness during the closing stages of the 1939 war led the writer to the originals from which this book has sprung. It was in the year 1900 that the late Dr Alexander Carmichael published his two volumes of *Carmina Gadelica* in Edinburgh in a limited edition. It made a great stir in the world of Celtic scholarship – 'hymns and incantations . . . orally collected in the Highlands and Islands of Scotland'. He set down the Gaelic text with a line by line translation on the opposite page – the work of most of his lifetime, long periods of which were spent among the people who retained this spoken literature. In 1928, sixteen years after his death, his daughter Elizabeth Catherine, the wife of Professor W. J. Watson of Edinburgh University, published a second and cheaper edition. In 1940 and 1941 two further volumes (from his grandfather's notes and papers) were issued by her son, Professor James Carmichael Watson, who held the chair of Celtic at Edinburgh University; before he could proceed further he lost his life in the Mediterranean in 1942 while serving with the Royal Navy. But a fifth volume was published in 1954, edited by Mr Angus Matheson of Glasgow University, with the material unexhausted still.

It is the poems of the first four volumes which

have here been done into verse for English readers, the translations of Dr Carmichael and his grandson being followed fairly closely.

Poems of the Western Highlanders contained no fewer than 535 poems and prayers. For reasons of space, it has only been possible to include less than one fifth of these in the present selection. The choice has been dictated largely by the format and the criteria governing the *Praying With . . .* series. Many poems had to be omitted because they were simply too long. Others were unsuitable for different reasons – there were some enchanting animal poems, work songs and healing charms which, however delightful, have no place in a book of prayers. Several prayers and blessings, collected from different locations, were so similar that it would have been unnecessarily repetitious to include them all.

The final selection therefore consists of approximately one hundred prayers, praises and blessings, which reflect the particular spirit of Celtic Christianity and which can, often with little or no adaptation, be used perfectly well by modern day Christians in our very different world of the late twentieth century. They are concerned with the basics of human life – with bodily needs, the daily round, our fears and temptations and our need for security, with family love and friendship. No attempt has been made to keep to McLean's original order and arrangement, but the prayers have been grouped into categories more convenient for practical use. The number which follows each prayer refers to the numbering in *Poems of the Western Highlanders*.

We are grateful to Mrs Margaret McLean for allowing us to publish this selection from her late husband's work, thus making it once again available to a new generation of readers.

Triangle/SPCK
1988

Introduction

From the original Introduction by
G. R. D. McLean to *Poems of the Western Highlanders*

The visitor to the Highlands of Scotland, whether he goes by road, by railway, or by sea, is at once struck by the majestic range of the hills and mountains. To travel from Glasgow by Loch Lomond through Glen Coe and the Great Glen, to go from Stirling to Loch Awe and the Pass of Brander, to take the North Road or the Highland Railway from Perth by Killiecrankie to Inverness and beyond, is to pass through a stretch of country unrivalled in Europe. To one who has never before done so, the first sight is breathtaking. In the same way the archipelagoes of the Hebrides are something not to be forgotten.

These poems have some of this about them; they unfold the secrets of the people of the hills and islands to the eye. Where known, the place in which a poem was recited is given; most come from the Outer Isles – the sandy, treeless, marshy, rocky, furthest Hebrides – for it was there that Dr Carmichael was living during some years of his collecting.

Some of the poems have clearly an ancient origin; distinctly pre-Christian elements may be traced in them. Since all the material in the first volumes was transcribed from the 'sixties up to the close of the last century from persons almost invariably advanced in years, none of it can now be less than one hundred and fifty years old; and most must go back at the least to before 1745 and the break-up of the Highlands. Dr Carmichael's own claim is that the bulk goes back with tolerable exactness a further hundred years to the first half of the seventeenth century. So far the pedigree is reliable. But it is clear that much older elements are present.

Whatever the date, in bulk the *Carmina Gadelica* poems represent what Dr D. J. Macleod described as 'the biggest sum of literature in any Western European language handed down by word of mouth'. The wonderful thing is that they recreate a whole life and civilisation that is now past, while the religion they breathe has largely become merged in more formalised expression. They present a pastoral and sea-going race, with its celebrations, its 'guisers' or carollers, its customs, its seedtime and its harvest; its games, its difficulties, its scourges, prejudices, and fears; its simple but deep faith, coming sometimes near to a pantheism of earth, living creature, and element.

'Gaelic oral literature', wrote Dr Carmichael, 'has been disappearing during the last three centuries. It is now becoming meagre in quantity, inferior in quality, and greatly isolated.' But he does also say: 'Although in decay, these poems are in verse of high order, with metre, rhythm, assonance, alliteration, and every quality to please the ear and to instruct the mind.' Professor Watson says much the same thing: 'It is as literature, and noble literature, that these poems make their highest appeal; and he is little to be envied in whom it wakens no response. They have beauties and graces which are at once apparent, and others they yield only to a faithful lover.'

Dr Carmichael laments that he was unable to convey 'the simple dignity, the charming grace, and the passionate devotion of the original'. Nor was it possible for him to reproduce fully the features he enumerated above; nor is it possible to render them adequately in any translation. But there does remain a verbal quality which corresponds to the disciplined repetitions of developed Celtic art – oral repetitions of an exactness that parallels the scholar's exactness of text in a manuscript.

Fortunately something of their musical quality has been expressed in the great collection of material edited and published as the *Songs of the Hebrides* by the late Mrs Marjorie Kennedy-Fraser and the Reverend Dr Kenneth Macleod. Their work on a more local scale has been amplified considerably by Miss Margaret Fay Shaw (Mrs J. L. Campbell) in her *Folksongs and Folklore of South Uist*. It is therefore possible to know of the sound of this poetry. But, except musically, the *Carmina Gadelica* go far beyond these works.

They are offered therefore mainly for the original purpose for which the bulk of them was composed, namely their values of religious expression. They have an especial worth in their nearness in spirit and tradition to the early Christian religion of North Britain, and in their wonderful mirror of the faith of a people who were of necessity individualists, and whose church was nature. Learned by heart and passed on from generation to generation, these are the prayers and hymns of the nomadic Christian missionaries, similar to those heard by the first converts of the Saxon Church in Northumbria and Mercia.

It is easy to see the later traces both of Romanism (very prominent, though very Highland) and of Protestantism. The late Frank Adam, the modern historiographer of the Highlands, held the view that the clans, with notable exceptions like the Campbells, adhered in spirit to the Celtic Church and inclined to a modified Romanism and to Episcopalianism rather than to the uncompromising Calvinism of the Kirk. The intoning also of these poems was that of the Celtic Church, similar to and dissimilar from Gregorian chanting. All that has survived has survived the Roman Church, the Reformation, the Risings, the Disruption, the emigrations, the evictions, the schools, and the ages of reason and science. But it is still possible to discern the spirit of that Columban church in these poems to which even now they are a more durable monument than the stones and crosses of Iona which they (or something very like them) inspired.

The unique feature here is that for the most part the poems are private; they reveal what is not usually revealed to strangers and outsiders. This fact, of itself, commands a respect. They do not include the heroic and public literature of the *ceilidh* which owes so much to Campbell of Islay and to Hector Maclean, and which first won for the Highlands their place in European folklore.

A traditional rhymed verse has been chosen to present these poems in English; above all this is traditional poetry. Fidelity to the original has been a primary aim, and sometimes also to its metre. The work entailed achieving a rough self-taught Gaelic, for first attempts through translation only, under an impulsion of Keats' 'On first looking into Chapman's Homer', were both unsatisfactory and inaccurate.

Study of the poems reveals certain things. Two great religious conceptions, peculiar to the Celtic Church, the one a theme, the one a practice, are discovered. There is upon occasion an almost word-for-word identity between Highland and Western Irish versions of evening prayers – survivals only upon the fringes or within the recesses of the Celtic world – which perpetuates a striking and original sacramental contribution. This is the remarkable 'lying-down' theme, an extension of the Communion and Eucharist of the Last Supper to cover the hospitality afforded by God and Christ and the Holy Spirit to life's traveller or pilgrim; God is regarded both in himself and in his Three Persons as a Chief and *Ard Righ*, with personal ties to his people. It is after the manner of a chieftain, of a hero, or of a prince of royal feasting – a link with the world of the saga and the heaven of the nobles, and a more full version of the Communion and Agape of the Son of God. There is an immanence here; it is quite without parallel in English Christianity.

The second contribution is the ministry of the soul-friend, also without parallel. The diminution of the *anam-chara*, soul-friend, into confessor is Irish rather than Highland. In the Hebrides especially the soul-friend remained lay, although he had a priestly function. His task was to sing the 'soul-peace' slowly over a dying person, leading the other watchers; he made the sign of the cross with his right thumb over the lips of the stricken one. Afterwards the soul-friend retained a place of special affection in the family.

The Highlander from rude experience was unaccustomed to look for security. He did look for protection, and of various sorts. He liked his spells and charms, his talismans, those minor Acropolis-presences or Jerusalem-citadels that serve to focus the tenacity of strong, simple people. These were for the unpredictable or imponderable and awful dangers of life and war. And then he was deeply aware of the day-to-day perils of dangerous living, which his so often was. Here the shield of God was very real to him; here the little ritual of encompassment (*caim*) gave comfort and assurance; here the 'good spirits' – the saints and the angels – were called in to aid. And then he was sufficiently a man of God to be conscious of the abysses of mortal jeopardy into which his soul could fall. Here self-dedication and prayer were his strong allies.

If protection prayers are defensive, good wishes attack the dangers of life without and within. The animal life, the elements, the hazards, the teeming seas are miraculously converted into immense sources of spiritual power – the wildness, almost savagery, of this western world harnessed under God to the life of man.

But everything in Highland life was orientated to God – even the tartan and kilt was apparently of ecclesiastical origin. The priest, when celebrating the Christian mysteries, was permitted a garment or vestment of eight colours – one more than the *Ard Righ* or High King; thereafter six colours for great chiefs and less down the scale, all depending on some fifty or sixty roots, plants, flowers, lichens, juices, trees, and barks, and combinations of these, which made the wonderful range of vegetable dyes used.

Law too was largely ecclesiastical in origin – it

stemmed from 'the four chief laws of Ireland', the law of Patrick against the slaying of clerics, the law of Darí against cattle-stealing, the law of Adamman against the slaying of women, the law of Sunday against travelling then. Even in fighting (and over a number of centuries the Highlands are not without their atrocities, which were recognised as such), the prevailing tradition was of a noble ferocity.

Economically the sea was essential, for the soil was insufficient. Highland sea-power fluctuated, and it diminished earlier than other springs of life – the warning of what was to come. It was never stable. The Celtic Church was compelled to retreat before maritime marauders; nor did Norwegian suzerainty supply a sufficiently constant resin of sustenance, with the result that the defeat at Largs became ultimately inevitable. The period of independence under the Lords of the Isles, like the golden age of the Children of Israel, was fitfully glorious. And by degrees the sea-power of the clans, once divided, would be plucked and impaired by more consistent and better supported forces. By the sixteenth century's close the clans were much less able to launch out, and their sea-power was virtually gone. After Culloden there was not a vestige and no maritime ability to retain the Prince in retreat. Whether the Highlander realised that he never fully mastered the sea is doubtful; but the poems show that he understood it and came to terms with it.

Otherworldliness is represented in concrete form by the sun, the moon, the planets, and the stars. They were connected with earlier faiths; they have become loosely interwoven into the Celtic Christian tradition. The sun survives only as an adjunct of the Father's glory (the eye of God); the moon remains, mostly because no theology was attached to her and she does not impinge on the Creeds. The planets and the stars are swallowed up in the angels and saints, the holy ones, the household and company of heaven.

Bird and animal life was minutely observed and interpreted. The tradition was Columban. Plant-life was primarily a marvellously spread world of healing, of colouring for wool, of fodder and uses for stock, of the gifts of God the Creator. The tradition was of St Beatan and of all the Macbeths, Beatons, Bethunes, Livingstones, and others of the healing hand.

Evening prayers are the most interesting of any, partly from the 'lying down' theme already mentioned, partly because the ancient origins and forms happen to be the clearest. Archbishop Bernard observed that the structure of the great Lorica of St Patrick 'seems to have been followed more or less closely in the composition of later charms of a similar character'. Other early examples of loricas or breast-plates begin in the same way 'with an invocation of the Trinity', and then call upon 'saints and angels', finally enumerating in detail 'the parts of the human body which might be subject to injury. . . . The opening invocation of the Trinity . . . is undoubtedly a very ancient Celtic form' (Bernard and Atkinson, *The Irish Liber Hymnorum*, ii, pp. 210–11). For it will be noticed that a structure of prayer exists. Openings are made, followed by the necessary special adaptation – a similar opening introduces a prayer of baptism and a prayer of sea-voyaging. It is possible therefore still to utilise this prayer language for many purposes today.

Prayer language is the achievement of these poems. The variations and combinations of the titles ascribed to the Deity are numerous; upon occasion there is confusion of the Three Persons of the Trinity; the same titles are even sometimes accorded outside, to St Mary and St Michael particularly. To the Gael, God is clearly of nature, of humanity, and of the spirit; and in all these aspects he is real, tremendous, near, loving, and within. He is the *De nan dul*, the God of life, the living God, the God of all.

He is revealed through the words and personalities of the many reciters, known and unknown, and through Dr Alexander Carmichael himself, to whom it is not possible to pay adequate tribute and of whom no one speaks or writes but with respect and affection.

One problem raises itself. How was it that such an extraordinarily strong and deep faith should prove inadequate and fail to triumph and survive? A full answer would be hard to give; nor would it be altogether true that it was inadequate or failed. But partially it is true to say that some of its trappings were too vulnerable to the modern onslaught of reason, utilitarianism, scientific knowledge, and economic necessity. The fairies and spirits had to go; with them went much of the religious faith and practice with which they were sometimes confused. And yet it is still a tremendous spiritual achievement, capable even of a revivification in these days of a latter Dispersion.

G. R. D. McLean
1961

GREAT GOD
OF ALL GODS

The Creed Prayer

O great God of all gods, I believe
That thou art the Father eternal of all life above;
O great God of all gods, I believe
That thou art the Father eternal of goodness and love.

O great God of all gods, I believe
That thou art the Father eternal of each holy one;
O great God of all gods, I believe
That thou art the Father eternal of each lowly one.

O great God of all gods, I believe
That thou art the Father eternal of each clan of men;
O great God of all gods, I believe
That thou art the Father eternal of earth of our ken.

Chief and God of the hosts, I believe
That thou art the creator and maker of heav'n on high,
That thou art the creator and maker of soaring sky,
That thou art the creator of oceans that under lie.

Chief and God of the hosts, I believe
That thou art the creator and warper of my soul's thread,
Thou my body's creator from dust and earth-ashes' bed,
Thou my body's breath-giver and thou my soul's domain
    bred.

O Father, bless to me my members,
O Father, bless my soul and being,
O Father, bless to me life's embers,
O Father, bless belief and seeing.

Father eternal, Chief of hosts, I believe
That my soul thou with thine own Spirit of healing didst
 mend,
And thou thy belov'd Son in covenant for me didst send,
And thou the blest blood of thy Son for my soul didst
 expend.
  Father eternal, Chief of all, I believe
That thou at baptising the Spirit of grace didst extend.

  Father eternal, Chief of mankind,
  Enwrap my body and soul entwined,
  Safeguard me tonight in thy love shrined,
  The saints' aid tonight my shelter kind.

  For thou has brought me up from the night
  Unto this morning's most gracious light,
  Great joy unto my soul to provide,
  And excelling good to do beside.

  O Jesu Christ, all thanks be to thee
  For the many gifts bestowed on me,
  For each sea and land, each day, each night,
  For each mild, each fresh, each weather bright.

I am giving thee worship with my whole life every hour,
  I am giving thee assent with my whole power,
With my fill of tongue's utterance I am giving thee praise,
  I am giving thee honour with my whole lays.

I am giving thee reverence with my whole knowledge
    upcaught,
        I am giving thee offering with my whole thought,
I am giving extolling with my whole good intent's flood,
        I am giving thee meekness in the Lamb's blood.

I am giving thee loving with my devotion's whole art,
        I am giving kneeling with my whole desire,
I am giving thee liking with my whole beating of heart,
        I am giving affection with my sense-fire;
I am giving mine existing with my mind and its whole,
        O God of all gods, I am giving my soul.

        My thought, my deed, my word, and my will,
        My mind, my brain, my state and my way,
        I beseech thee to keep me from ill,
        To keep from hurt and from harm today;
        To keep me from grieving and from plight,
        In thy love's nearness to keep this night.

        O may God shield me, and may God fill,
        O may God watch me, and may God hold;
        O may God bring me where peace is still,
        To the King's land, eternity's fold.

        Praise to the Father, praise to the Son,
        Praise to the Spirit, the Three in One.

2 *Morar*

Christmas Carol

Ho to the King! blessed is he!
Ho to the King! blessed is he!
Ho to the King of whom we sing!
    Ho! ro! joy let there be!

This night is the eve of greatest birth,
    Born is the Son of Mary Maid,
The soles of his feet have touched the earth,
    Son of glory above displayed,
    Heaven and earth to him aglow
        As he comes below,
    Ho! ro! joy let there be!

Heavenly joy and peace upon earth,
    Behold his feet have reached the place;
O worship the King, hail the Lamb's birth,
    King of the virtues, Lamb of grace,
    Ocean and earth to him alit
        As he doeth it,
    Ho! ro! joy let there be!

The gleam of distance, the gleam of sand,
    Roar of waves with a tide that sings
To tell us that Christ is born at hand,
    Saving Son of the King of kings,
    Sun on the mountains high ashine
        Reveals him divine,
    Ho! ro! joy let there be!

The earth and the spheres together shine,
    The Lord God opes the starry floor;
Haste, Son of Mary, assistance mine,
    Thou Christ of hope, and joy's wide Door,
    On hills and ranges, golden Sun,
       Behold, it is done!
      Ho! ro! joy let there be!

28   *Lewis*

The Star-Kindler

The Kindler of the starry fires
Behold, cloud-pillowed like desires,
And all the aery feathered quires
      Are lauding him.

With heavenly music down he came
Forth from the Father of his Name,
While harp and lyre in song acclaim
      Applauding him.

O Christ, thou refuge of my love,
Why lift not I thy fame above?
When saints and angels full enough
      Are songing thee.

O sweet MacMary of all grace,
How glist'ring white thy pure fair face,
How rich the joyful pasture place
      Belonging thee!

O Christ my loved beyond the flood,
O Christ, thou of the Holy Blood,
By day and night outswell my bud
      Of praising thee.

23   *Morar and Barra*

The Voice of Thunder

O God of the elemental might,
O God of the mysterious height,
O God of the stars and cloudsprings bright,
  O King of kings to bestow!
  O King of kings to bestow!

Thy joy the joy of the raindrops' play,
Thy light the light of the lightning's spray,
Thy war the war of the heavenly fray,
  Thy peace the peace of the bow,
  Thy peace the peace of the bow.

Thy pain the pain of groaning and clash,
Thy love the love of the sudden flash,
That lasts for aye like the music's crash,
  Till the end of ends below,
  Till the end of ends below.

Thou pourest thy grace, refreshing shower,
Upon men in grief and duress hour,
Upon men in straits and danger's power,
  Without cease or stint to show,
  Without cease or stint to show.

Thou Son of Mary of Paschal feat,
Thou Son of Mary of death's defeat,
Thou Son of Mary of grace replete,
  Who wast and art, shalt be so
  With the ebb and with the flow;
    Who wast and art, shalt be so,
    With the ebb and with the flow!

450

Sunrise

The eye of God, the God who is great,
The eye of the God of glory's state,
The eye of the King of hosts that strive,
The eye of the King of all alive,
Pour out as time and moments go,
Pour out on us thy gen'rous flow,
   On us thy gentle gen'rous flow.

Thou sun of joy, glory to thee,
To thee be glory, O thou sun,
Face of the God of life to see,
Face of the morning rising one,
   To thee be glory, O thou sun.

451   *South Uist and Mingulay of Barra*

Jesus-Praise

It were as easy, Lord, for thee
As to wither the sapling new
Anew to green the withered tree
Were it thy will the thing to do,
  O Jesu, Jesu, Jesu,
  Unto whom all praise is due.

There is no plant in all the land
But blooms replete with thy virtue,
Each form in all the sweeping strand
With joy replete thou dost endue,
  O Jesu, Jesu, Jesu,
  Unto whom all praise is due.

All life that is within the sea,
In river every dwelling thing,
All in the firmament that be
Thy goodness overflowing sing,
  O Jesu, Jesu, Jesu,
  Unto whom all praise is due.

Each single star fixed in the sky,
Each bird arising on the wing,
They that beneath the sun do lie
Thy goodness all proclaiming sing,
  O Jesu, Jesu, Jesu,
  Unto whom all praise is due.

326   Harris

Doxology

As it was, as it is, and as it shall be
Evermore, God of grace, God in Trinity!
With the ebb, with the flow, ever it is so,
God of grace, O Trinity, with the ebb and flow.

449   Barra

THIS DAY

Prayer this Day

My prayer to thee, O God, pray I this day,
Voice I this day in thy mouth's voicing way,
As hold the men of heaven this day I hold,
Spend I this day as spends thine own household,
Under thy laws, O God, this day I go,
As saints in heaven pass pass I this day so.

Thou loving Christ who hangedst on the tree,
Each day, each night, thy compact mindeth me;
Lie down or rise unto thy cross I cede,
In life and death thou health and peace indeed.

Each day thy mercies' source let me recall,
Gentle, gen'rous bestowing on me all;
Each day in love to thee more full be I
For love to me that thou didst amplify.

From thee it came, each thing I have received,
From love it comes, each thing my hope conceived,
Thy bounty gives each thing that gives me zest,
Of thy disposing each thing I request.

God holy, loving Father, of the word
Everlasting, this living prayer be heard:
Understanding lighten, my will enfire,
Begin my doing and my love inspire,
My weakness strengthen, enfold my desire.

Cleanse heart, faith confirm, sanctify my soul,
Circle my body, and my mind keep whole;
As from my mouth my prayer upriseth clear,
May I feel in my heart that thou art here.

And, O God of life, do thou grant to me
That thou at my breast, at my back shalt be,
That thou give my needs as befits the gold,
The above-world crown to us promise-told.

And, Father beloved, grant thou that to me,
From whom each thing that is outfloweth free,
No tie too strict, no tie too dear between
Myself and this beneath-world here be seen.

O my God, in thee all my hope I set,
Father of the heav'ns, my living hope yet,
My great hope with thyself that I may be
In the far world that cometh finally.

Father, Son, Spirit, Holy Trinity,
Three in One Person and the One in Three,
Infinite and perfect, world without end,
Changeless through endless life, let praise ascend.

94

From the Darkness

O gentle Christ, ever thanks to thee,
That thou from the dark hast raised me free
And from the coldness of last night's space
To the gentle light of this day's grace.

O God of all creatures, praise to thee,
As to each life thou hast poured on me,
My wish, my word, my sense, my man praise,
My thought, my deed, my fame, and my ways.

252

The Lighthouse Prayer

O God, who from last night's sweet rest dost me convey
To the light of joy of the day that is today,
From the new light of this day be thou bringing me,
Unto the light of guidance of eternity,
    From the new light today be thou bringing me
    Unto the guiding light of eternity.

434   Monks' Heiskir of North Uist

Rising Prayer

Thou King of the moon and of the sun,
Of the stars thou lov'd and fragrant King,
Thou thyself knowest our needs each one,
O merciful God of everything.

Each day that our moving steps we take,
Each hour of awakening, when we know
The dark distress and sorrow we make
To the King of hosts who loved us so;

Be with us through the time of each day,
Be with us through the time of each night,
Be with us ever each night and day,
Be with us ever each day and night.

87

Morning Thanksgiving

That I have ris'n today, O God, the thanks be unto thee,
    To the rising of this life itself again;
O God of every gift, to thine own glory may it be,
    To the glory of my soul likewise a gain.

O great God, unto my soul give thine aid and make it full
    With the great aiding of thine own mercy whole;
Even as I am covering all my body with the wool,
    With the shadow of thy wing cover my soul.

God, be helping mine avoiding every sin that life fills,
    And my forsaking the cause of sinful ways;
And as flees the mist of morning on the crest of the hills,
    May there clear off from my soul each evil haze.

89

The Pilgrim's Hope

I bathe my face in water fresh,
As the sun his nine rays doth spread,
As Mary washed her Son's fair flesh
In the generous milk white-shed.

May mercy be my lips' attire,
May kindness to my face be lent,
May chasteness be on my desire,
And wisdom be in mine intent.

Love Ma.y laid her one Son on
May all the world give unto me;
Love Jesus-giv'n to Baptist John
Grant I give to each one I see.

Son of God, be at the outset,
Son of God, be surety, friend;
Son of God, make straight my way yet,
Son of God at my seeking's end.

69   Morar

The Morning Dedication

Let thanks, O God, be unto thee,
From yesterday who broughtest me
The morning of today to see,
Joy everlasting to earn whole
With good intention for my soul.
For every gift of peace to me,
Thoughts, words, deeds, and desires from thee
Each one bestowed, I dedicate.
And I beseech, I supplicate
That thou may'st keep me from offence,
Tonight my aiding and defence,
For the sake of thy wounding red,
With thine offering of grace outspread.
Let thanks, O God, be unto thee.

90   North Uist

Morning Prayer

O Jesus Christ, all thanks be to thee,
Who hast brought me safely through last night,
To the morning joy of this day's light,
To win everlasting life for me,
Through the blood that thou didst shed for me.

O God, for ever praise be to thee,
For the blessings thou bestow'st on me –
For my food, my work, my health, my speech,
For all the good gifts bestowed on each,
O God, for ever praise be to thee.

I pray thee now to shield me from woe,
From sinning, this night to consecrate,
God of the poor, and I poor and low,
O Christ of the wounds, thy wisdom great
Along with thy grace on me bestow.

May the Holy One make claim on me,
And protect me on the land and sea,
Step by step leading me on my way
To the City of e'erlasting day,
Peace of the City that lasts for aye.

158   Lochaber

Each Day and Night

Each day in justice let me speak,
Each day thy chastening marks, O God, display,
Each day in wisdom let me speak,
Each night at peace with thee, at peace each day;

Each day thy mercy's causes store,
Each day may I compose to thee a song,
Each day give heedance to thy law,
Each day string out, O God, thy praises strong;

Each day love let me give to thee,
Each night, O Jesu, grant I do the same,
Each day and night laud give to thee
Or dark or light, for goodness of thy Name,
Or dark or light,
Each day and night.

409   Barra

Somerled's Supplication

O Being of life! O Being of peace!
O Being of time, and time without cease!
O Being, infinite eternity!
O Being, infinite eternity!

In good means of life be thou keeping me,
In all good intending, o keeping be,
Be keeping me always in good estate,
Far better than I know to supplicate,
     O better than I know to supplicate!

Be shepherding me for all this day long,
Relieve my distress, relieve me from wrong,
Enfold me this night with thine arms' embrace,
And pour upon me thy bountiful grace,
     O pour upon me thy bountiful grace!

My speaking and words do thou guard for me,
And strengthen for me my love, charity,
Illumine for me the stream I must o'er,
And succour thou me when I pass death's door,
     O succour thou me when I pass death's door!

95   Benbecula

Life-Consecration

Jesu MacMary, have mercy upon us;
Jesu MacMary, thy peace be upon us;
   Where we shall longest be,
   With us and for us be,
   Amen, eternally.

Jesu MacMary, at dawn-tide, the flowing,
Jesu MacMary, at ebb-tide, the going;
   When our first breath awakes,
   Life's day when darkness takes,
Merciful God of all, mercy bestowing,
   With us and for us be,
   Merciful Deity,
   Amen, eternally.

Condition and lot, to thee make them holy,
Condition and lot, to thee take them wholly,
   King of all kings that be,
   God of all things that be,
   Amen, eternally.

Our rights and our means, to thee make them holy,
Our rights and our means, to thee take them wholly,
   King of all kings that be,
   God of all things that be,
   Amen, eternally.

Our body and heart, to thee make them holy,
Our body and heart, to thee take them wholly,
   King of all kings that be,
   God of all things that be,
   Amen, eternally.

Each body and heart, the whole of each being,
Each day, each night also, thine overseeing,
   King of all kings that be,
   God of all things that be,
   Amen, eternally.

319   Harris

Thoughts

'Tis God's will I would do,
My own will I would rein;
Would give to God his due,
From my own due refrain;
God's path I would pursue,
My own path would disdain;

For Christ's death would I care,
My own death duly weighed;
Christ's pain my silent prayer,
My God-love warmer made;
'Tis Christ's cross I would bear,
My own cross off me laid;

Repentance I would make,
Repentance early choose;
Rein for my tongue would take,
Rein for my thoughts would use;

God's judgment would I mind,
My own judgment close-scanned;
Christ's freedom seizing bind,
My own freedom in hand;
Christ's love close-scanned would find,
My own love understand.

71

The New Year

God bless to me the new day that is here,
Nor ever yet before designed for me;
It is to bless thy countenance so dear
This time, O God, thou givest me to see.

O bless thou unto me my seeing eye,
And mine eye bless each one that it doth see;
My neighbour I will bless who liveth nigh,
My neighbour give his blessing unto me.

O God, give me a heart of cleanliness,
Nor be I from thy watching eye offstood;
And unto me my wife and children bless,
Bless unto me my stock and livelihood.

364   Skye, North Uist and elsewhere

Prayer for the Day

Do thou, O God, bless unto me
    Each thing mine eye doth see;
Do thou, O God, bless unto me
    Each sound that comes to me;
Do thou, O God, bless unto me
    Each savour that I smell;
Do thou, O God, bless unto me
    Each taste in mouth doth dwell;
Each sound that goes unto my song,
    Each ray that guides my way,
Each thing that I pursue along,
    Each lure that tempts to stray,
The zeal that seeks my living soul,
The Three that seek my heart and whole,
    The zeal that seeks my living soul,
    The Three that seek my heart and whole.

310   *Gairloch*

THE PATH I WALK

A Journey Prayer

This day to me, God, do thou bless,
This very night, God, blessing give,
Thou God of grace, o do thou bless
All days and all the times I live;
    Thou God of grace, o do thou bless
    All days and all the times I live.

God, bless the path I walk above,
God, bless the earth beneath my toes;
God, bless me, give to me thy love,
O God of gods, bless rest, repose;
    God, bless me, give to me thy love,
    O God of gods, bless my repose.

6   *Benbecula*

The Travel-Shield of God

Almighty Lord, thou God of might,
  Shield me this night and sustain,
Almighty Lord, thou God of might,
  This night and each eve again.

Sain me and save me from mischief whole,
  And from sin save me and sain,
Sain me my body and my soul,
  Each dark and each light again.

Bless me the land my hope doth prize,
  Bless me the thing faith shall see,
Bless me the thing my love descries,
  God of life, bless what I be.

Bless the journey whereon I go,
  And bless the ground under me,
Bless the matter I seek to know,
  Glory-King, bless what I be.

76

East or West

May the everlasting Father throw
     His shield to shade you
Every east and west that you may go,
     His shield to aid you.

423

Fear by Night

God before me, God behind,
God above me, God below;
On the path of God I wind,
God upon my track doth go.

Who is there upon the shore?
Who is there upon the wave?
Who is there on sea-swell roar?
Who is there by door-post stave?
Who along with us doth stand?
God and Lord on either hand.

I am here abroad, without,
I am here in want, in need,
I am here in pain, in doubt,
I am here in straits indeed,
I am here alone, afraid,
O God, grant to me thine aid.

402

The Roadmaker

God be shielding thee by each dropping sheer,
God make every pass an opening appear,
God make to thee each road a highway clear,
   And may he take thee in the clasp
       Of his own two hands' grasp.

394

By Upland and Brae

On every steep to thee God's shielding shade,
On every climb to thee may Christ give aid,
On every rise the Spirit's filling made,
Thy way by upland or by plainland braeed.

403

The Pilgrim's Aiding

May God be with thee in every pass,
Jesus be with thee on every knoll,
Spirit be with thee by water's roll,
   On headland, on ridge, and on grass;

Each sea and land, each moor and each mead,
Each eve's lying-down, each rising's morn,
In the wave-trough, or on foam-crest borne,
   Each step which thy journey doth lead.

68   South Uist

Sea Blessing

God the Father almighty, whose kindness cheers,
O Jesu the Son of the sorrows and tears,
O thine aiding aid, Holy Spirit, endears!

The Three-One e'er living, great, lasting, o'erhead,
Who across the Red Sea the Israelites led,
And Jonah to land from the sea-monster sped,

Who led Paul with his company setting sail,
Forth from the sea-stress, from the wave-torment's flail,
From the storm that was great, from foul-weather gale,

When the tempest poured on the Lake Galilee,
The disciples cried out in their misery,
And thou Jesu of sleeping didst still the sea.

O sain us, set us free, and sanctify best,
On our helm, O King of the elements, rest,
And steer us in peace to our voyage's quest.

Gentle winds, kindly, pleasant, fragrant to waft,
Not an eddy, nor swirl, nor whirl for our craft,
But safe let her ride and unscathed fore and aft.

All things of thy bounty, O God, we beseech,
For thy will so and word accordingly teach.

441   North Uist

Ship Consecration

HELMSMAN	Be the ship blest.
CREW	By God the Father blest.
HELMSMAN	Be the ship blest.
CREW	And by God the Son blest.
HELMSMAN	Be the ship blest.
CREW	By God the Spirit blest.
ALL	God the Father, ·
	And God the Son,
	God the Spirit,
	Blessing give blest,
	Be the ship blest.
HELMSMAN	What can afear
	With God the Father near?
CREW	Naught can afear.
HELMSMAN	What can afear
	And God the Son is near?
CREW	Naught can afear.
HELMSMAN	What can afear
	And God the Spirit near?
CREW	Naught can afear.
ALL	God the Father
	And God the Son,
	God the Spirit,
	Be with us here
	And ever near.

HELMSMAN	What care is bred,
	Being of all o'erhead?
CREW	No care is bred.
HELMSMAN	What care is bred,
	The King of all o'erhead?
CREW	No care is bred.
HELMSMAN	What care is bred,
	Spirit of all o'erhead?
CREW	No care is bred.

ALL   Being of all,
The King of all,
Spirit of all,
Over our head
Eternal fall,
  Near to us sure
  For evermore.

443   South Uist

The Helmsman

God of the elements, glory to thee
For the lantern-guide of the ocean wide;
On my rudder's helm may thine own hand be,
And thy love abaft on the heaving sea.

448

A Sailor's Prayer

Thou Being who Jonah didst safely land
Out from the bag of the sow of the sea,
Bring thou myself to the beckoning strand
With lading and ship entrusted to me.

444

GIVE US, O GOD . . .

The Gates of the Kingdom

Give us, O God, the needs the body feels,
   Give us, God, the need-things of the soul;
Give us, O God, the balm which body heals,
   Give us, God, the soul-balm which makes whole.

Bliss give us, O God, of repentance-ease,
   Bliss give us, God, of forgiveness sought,
Away from us wash thou corruption's lees,
   From us wipe the blush of unclean thought.

O great God, thou who art upon the throne,
   Give to us the heart repentance true,
Forgiveness give us of the sin we own –
   The sin inborn and the sin we do.

Give us, O God, a yearning that is strong,
   And the crown of glory of the King;
Give us the safe home, God, for which we long
   In thy kingdom's lovely gates to sing.

May Michael, archangel warrior white,
   Keep down hostile demons of the fall;
May Jesus Christ MacDavid guide our flight
   And give lodging in his peace-bright hall.

54   Benbecula

The Meal

Give us, O God, our morning bread,
The soul by body nourishéd;
Give us, O God, the perfect bread,
Sufficiently at evening fed.

Give us, O God, milk-honey yield,
The strength and cream of fragrant field;
God, give us rest, our eyelids sealed,
Thy Rock of covenant our shield.

Give us this night the living fare,
This night the saving drink be there;
This night, for heaven to prepare,
Give us the cup of Mary fair.

Be with us ever night and day,
In light and darkness, be our stay,
With us, abed or up, alway,
In talk, in walk and when we pray.

49

Grace before Food

Be with me, O God, at breaking of bread,
And be with me, O God, when I have fed;
Naught come to my body my soul to pain,
O naught able my contrite soul to stain.

4   *Benbecula*

Thanks after Food

O God, all thanks be unto thee,
O God, all praise be unto thee,
O God, worship be unto thee,
For all that thou hast given me.

As thou didst give my body life
To earn for me my drink and food,
So grant to me eternal life
To show forth all thy glory good.

Through all my life grant to me grace,
Life grant me at the hour of death;
God with me at my leaving breath,
God with me in deep currents' race.

O God, in the breath's parting sigh,
O, with my soul in currents deep,
Sounding the fords within thy keep,
Crossing the deep floods, God be nigh.

5   *Benbecula*

God of the Sea

O God of the heaving sea,
Give the wave fertility,
Weed for enriching the ground,
Our life-giving pouring sound.

300   Iona and elsewhere

Before Prayer

The Father who created me
With eye benign beholdeth me;
The Son who dearly purchased me
With eye divine enfoldeth me;
The Spirit who so altered me
With eye refining holdeth me;
In friendliness and love the Three
Behold me when I bend the knee.

O God, through thine Anointed One,
The fullness of our needs be done –
Grant us towards God the love ordained,
Grant us towards man the love unfeigned;
Grant us the smile of God's good face,
Grant us God's wisdom and God's grace;
Grant us to fear and reverence still,
Grant in the world to do thy will
As done in heaven by saintly hands
And myriad of angelic bands;
Each day and night, each dawn and fall,
Grant us in kindness, Lord of all,
Thy nature's tincture at our call.

157   *Lochaber*

For Forgiveness

On this day, on this thy night,
   O God be with us, Amen.
On this thy day, on this thy night,
   To us and with us, Amen.

It is full clear within our sight
That since we came to this world's light
We have deserved thy wrath's despite;
   O God be with us, Amen.

O God of all, o thine own wrath,
Stretch, O God, thy forgiveness forth,
   To us forgiveness, Amen,
   Forgiveness with us, Amen,
   To us and with us, Amen.

Thine own forgiveness to us give,
Merciful God, by whom we live,
Merciful God of all, forgive,
   O God be with us, Amen,
   To us and with us, Amen.

Anything that to us is ill,
Or that may stand against us till
We come where is our longest day,
   Lighten it to us aright,
   O darken its ugly light,
   O banish it from our sight,
Forth from our heart chase it away,
For everlasting and for aye,
   Ever and ever, Amen.
For everlasting and for aye,
   Ever and ever, Amen,
   O God be with us, Amen.

318   Harris

Confession

Jesu, give unto me the forgiveness of sin,
Jesu, be mine erring not forgotten within,
Jesu, give me the grace of repentance's school,
Jesu, give me the grace of forgiveness in full,
Jesu, give me the grace of submissiveness due,
Jesu, give me the grace of sincerity true,
Jesu, give me the grace of humility's part,
My confession to make at this time from my heart,
At throne of confession condemnation to own
Lest condemnation I find at the judgement throne;
Jesu, give me the strength and the courage, alone
At throne of confession condemnation to own
Lest condemnation I find at the judgement throne.
More easy is a season of chastening to me
Than a descent unto death for eternity.
Jesu, give unto me all my guilt to confess
With the urgency of death's importunateness.

>   Jesu, take pity, o take pity on me,
>   Jesu, upon me have mercy, mercy whole,
>   Jesu, do thou take me, o take me to thee,
>   Jesu, give thou aid, o give aid to my soul.

>   Sin is of grief a cause, o a cause,
>   And a cause of sore anguish is death,
>   But repentance is of joy a cause
>   And the cleansing stream's life-giving breath.

O Shepherd, who leavest the ninety and nine,
Good Shepherd, who seekest the sheep that hath slipt,
The angels of heav'n will have joy that is mine
That in the confession-stirred pool I am dipt.

O my soul, lift up and rejoicing be,
God willeth for thee an atonement above,
Seize his hand while it is stretched out unto thee
To announce to thee an atonement of love.

Withdraw not thy hand O my God, from me here,
O Chief of the chiefs, o withdraw not thy hand,
For Lord Jesus Christ's sake my Saviour so dear,
That I go not to death's everlasting land.

322   *Lochaber*

For Grace

I am bending low my knee
In the eye of those who see,
Father who my life supplied,
Saviour Son who for me died,
Spirit who hath purified,
In desire and love to thee.

Be the blessing heaven-sent
Richly poured on penitent;
City-Prince of firmament,
O forbear thy punishment.

Grant us, Glory-Saviour dear,
God's affection, love and fear,
God's will to do always here
As above in heaven clear
Saints and angels do not cease;
Day and night give us thy peace,
    Give each day and night thy peace.

237   *Berneray of Barra*

The Pilgrim's Relief

Each one, O God, do thou relieve
In all his suffering on land or sea,
In grief, or wound, or in tears, receive,
To thy peaceful halls his leader be
As day doth fade.

I am weary and weak and chill,
Weary of travelling on land and sea,
Of crossing moor and the foam-white hill,
Grant peace anigh of thine ease to me
As day doth fade.

O my God's Father, lovéd one,
Let the care of my crying suffice;
With thee I would wish atonement done,
Through the witness and the ransom price
Which thy Son paid;

With Jesus to find restfulness
In the blest habitation of peace,
In the paradise of gentleness,
In the fairy-bower of release
Mercy-arrayed.

75

He who was Crucified

Thou who wert hanged upon the tree,
By people condemned, crucified there,
  Now that grown old and grey I be,
Pity, O God, my confession-prayer.

  I wonder not my sins are great,
I am a clattering cymbal poor,
  I was profane in youth's estate,
Forlorn in my ageing at the door.

  Those to whom God hath no desire
Are people who lie, people who swear;
  Fountain-tears, hot-springing as fire
Rather would he, and genuine prayer.

99   Lochalsh, Kintail and Harris

Death Prayer

O God, of thy wisdom do thou give,
O God, of thy mercy that I live,
Of thine abundance, O God, provide,
In face of each strait be thou my guide.

God, of thy holiness consecrate,
O God, of thine aiding aid my state,
Of thy surrounding, O God, invest,
And in my death's knot give of thy rest;
   O of thy surrounding to invest,
    And in my dying hour of thy rest!

259   South Uist

Happy Death

Thou God of salvation great, outpour
On my soul thy graces from above
As up the sun of the heights doth soar
And on my body outpours its love.

Needs must that I die and go to rest,
Nor know I where or when it will be;
But if of thy graces unpossest
So I am lost everlastingly.

Death of anointing, repentance due,
Death of joy, death of peacefulness giv'n;
Death of grace, death of forgiveness true,
Death that endows life with Christ and heav'n.

51

Death's Ford

O may the Father clasp you in his hand,
His fragrant loving clasp bring you to land,
Across the flooding torrent when you go
And when the stream of death doth blackly flow.

524

GOD MY LIFE-WHOLE

God my Guide

O God with thy wisdom be my guide,
God with justice chastising provide,
O God with thy mercy be mine aid,
God my protection with might arrayed.

O God with thy fullness be my fill,
God with thy shadow cloak shield me still,
God with thy grace my fullness be done,
For the sake of thine Anointed Son.

Jesu the Christ of King David's line,
Visiting One of the Temple shrine,
Sacrifice Lamb of the Garden pure,
Whose death did my salvation procure.

417   South Uist

Morning Protection

Be the eye of God between me and each eye,
Between me and each purpose God's purpose lie,
Be the hand of God between me and each hand,
Between me and each shield the shield of God stand,
God's desire between me and each desire be,
Be God's bridle between each bridle and me,
    And no man's mouth able to curse me I see.

Between me and each pain the pain of Christ show,
Between me and each love the love of Christ grow,
Between me and each dearness Christ's dearness stay,
Christ's kindness between me and each kindness aye,
Between me and each wish the wish of Christ found,
Between me and each will the will of Christ bound,
    And no venom can wound me, make me unsound.

Be the might of Christ between me and each might,
Be the right of Christ between me and each right,
Flow of the Spirit between me and each flow,
Between me and each lave the Spirit's lave go,
Between me and each bathe the Spirit's bathe clean,
    And to touch me no evil thing can be seen.

93

Rest Benediction

Bless to me, O God, the moon above my head,
Bless to me, O God, the earth on which I tread,
Bless to me, O God, my wife and children all,
Bless, O God, myself to whom their care doth fall;
    Bless to me my wife and children all,
Bless, O God, myself to whom their care doth fall.

Bless, O God, the thing on which mine eye doth rest,
Bless, O God, the thing to which my hope doth quest,
Bless, O God, my reason and what I desire,
Bless, thou God of life, o bless myself entire;
    Bless my reason and what I desire,
Bless, thou God of life, o bless myself entire.

Bless to me the partner of my love and bed,
Bless to me the handling of my hands outspread,
Bless to me, O God, my compass compassing,
Bless, o bless to me sleep-angel mine a-wing;
    Bless to me my compass compassing,
Bless, o bless to me sleep-angel mine a-wing.

176   Benbecula

The Soul's Healer

Healer thou of my soul,
  At eventide keep whole,
  Keep me at morning ray,
  Keep me at full noonday,
As on my rough course I fare.

Safeguard me and assist
  That this night I subsist,
  I am tired and astray,
  And so stumbling my way,
Shield thou from sin and from snare.

73

God's Aid

God to enfold,
God to surround,
God in speech-told,
God my thought-bound.

God when I sleep,
God when I wake,
God my watch-keep,
God my hope-sake.

God my life-whole,
God lips apart,
God in my soul,
God in my heart.

God Wine and Bread,
God in my death,
God my soul-thread,
God ever breath.

48

Before Me

Before me be thou a smooth way,
Above me be thou a star-guide,
Behind me o be thou keen-eyed,
For this day, this night, and for aye.

I weary and heavy am driv'n,
Lead me on to the angels' place;
'Twere time now I went for a space
To Christ's court and the peace of heav'n;

If only thou, God of life, give
Smooth peace for me, at my back near,
Be as star, as helmsman to steer,
From smooth rest till rising I live.

72

Jesus the Encompasser

Jesu! Only-begotten mine,
God the Father's Lamb sacrificed,
Thou didst give the body's blood-wine
From the grave-death to buy me right.
My shield, my encircler, my Christ, my Christ!
For each day, each night, for each dark, each light.
My shield, my encircler, my Christ, my Christ!
For each day, each night, for each dark, each light.

Jesu! uphold me and be nigh,
My triumph, treasure, thou art now.
When I lie down, when stand, be by,
Whenever I watch, when I sleep.
My aid, my encircler, MacMary thou!
My strength everlasting, MacDavid, keep;
My aid, my encircler, MacMary thou!
My strength everlasting, MacDavid keep.

124   *Barra*

The Holy Spirit

O Holy Ghost
Of pow'r the most,
Come down upon us and subdue;
From glory's place
In heaven space,
Thy light of brilliance shed as dew.

Lov'd Father One
To each bare son,
From whom all gifts and goodness flow,
Our hearts enshrine
With mercy's shine,
In mercy shield from harm and woe.

God, without thee
Naught can there be
Within man that can a price gain;
King of kings, lo!
Without thee so
Ne'er a sinless man without stain.

All on thee stayed,
Thou the best aid
Against the soul of wildest speech;
Food thou art sweet
O'er other meat;
Sustain and guide at all times each.

The stiff-joint knee,
O Healer, free,
'Neath thy wing warm heart's hardness lie;
The soul astray
Out of thy way,
O swing back his helm lest he die.

Each foul thing seen
Early make clean,
Each that is hard grace-soften through,
Each wound or blow
That pains us so,
Healer of healers, whole renew!

Thy people must
In thee place trust,
God, grant diligence to do it;
Help them each hour
With sev'nfold pow'r,
Thy gift, gen'rous Holy Spirit!

253

The Holy Ghost Distilling

May the Holy Ghost distilling,
   Down from heaven forth to ground,
Grant me aid and goodness filling,
   That my prayer be firmly bound
The King of life's great throne around.

May the Holy Ghost with blessing
   Wing the prayer I send as dove
In the fitting state and gracing
   Of thy holy will above,
O Lord my God of life and love.

Be I in God's love, God's dearness,
   Be I in God's will, God's sight,
Be I in God's choice, God's nearness,
   Be I in God's charge, God's might,
And be I in God's keep aright.

As thine angels fair, untiring,
   As thy saints, household entire,
They in heav'n above desiring,
   So on earth may I desire,
With Holy Ghost aflame in fire.

260

Chief of Chiefs

Chief of chiefs beyond my ken,
O Chief of chiefs, Amen.

God be with me lying down,
And God be with me rising,
In the sunlight flying down
God with me, supervising,
No joy nor any light without him,
Nor any light without him.

Christ be with me sleeping hours,
And Christ be with me waking,
Through all watches aiding powers,
Christ with me undertaking,
No day nor any night without him,
Nor any night without him.

God be with me to protect,
The Spirit there to strengthen,
Lord be with me to direct
As span of life doth lengthen,
No time, no year, no hope, no fear,
No age, no space, no work, no place,
No depth nor any height without him,
Nor any height without him.

Ever, evermore, Amen,
O Chief of chiefs, Amen.

204   *Kintail and Harris*

The Path of Right

With God be my walking this day,
With Christ be my walking this day,
With Spirit my walking this day,
The Threefold all-kindly my way;
Ho, ho, ho! the Threefold all-kindly I pray.

My shielding this day be from bane,
My shielding this night be from pain,
Ho, ho! soul and body, the twain,
By Father, Son, Spirit, amain;
By Father's, by Son's, and by Holy Ghost's sain.

The Father be he shielding me,
And be God the Son shielding me,
The Spirit be he shielding me,
As Three and as One let them be:
Ho, ho, ho! as Three and as One Trinity.

67

Afloat and Afield

I pray to God my petition and rite,
To Mary's Son, to the Spirit of right,
In distress to assist afloat, afield;
The Three to give succour, the Three to shield,
The Three to watch me by day and by night.

God and Jesus and the Spirit so pure,
Possess me, and shield me, assist me sure,
Order my path and before my soul go
In hollow, on hill, and on plain below,
Afloat, afield, the assisting Three sure.

God and Jesus, Holy Spirit of right,
Give shielding and saving to me in might,
As Three and as One, the great Trinity,
By my back, by my side, and by my knee,
As through the drear world-storm my steps alight.

396

The Three Everywhere

The Three who are over my head,
The Three who are under my tread,
The Three who are over me here,
The Three who are over me there,
The Three who are in the earth near,
The Three who are up in the air,
The Three who in heaven do dwell,
The Three in the great ocean swell,
   Pervading Three, o be with me.

432

The Three

In the Father's name,
And in the Son's name,
In the Spirit's name,
Three the same, One in name;

Father be my friend,
And Son be my friend,
Spirit be my friend,
Three to send and befriend.

God my holiness,
Christ my holiness,
Spirit holiness,
Three to bless, holiness.

Help of hope the Three,
Help of love the Three,
Help of sight the Three,
And my knee stumbling free,
From my knee stumbling free.

70

THIS NIGHTFALL

The Soul Petition

O Jesu, this nightfall,
Who dost fold-herd the poor,
Without sin thou at all
Who didst suffer full sore,
By the wicked's decree,
Crucified thou for me,

From ill be my safeguard,
And safeguard me from sin,
Save my body and ward,
Make me holy within,
O Jesu, this nightfall,
Nor leave me till light fall.

O endow me with might,
Virtue-Herdsman of light,
Do thou guide me aright,
Do thou guide me in might,
Thine, O Jesu, the might,
Keep me safe until light.

164   *Lochaber*

Nightfall

Come I this day to the Father of light,
Come I this day to the Son, morning bright,
Come I to the Holy Ghost great in might;
Come I this day with God, blessing to find,
Come I this day with Christ, promise to bind.
Come I with the Spirit of potion kind.

O God, and Spirit, and Jesu, the Three,
From the crown of my head, O Trinity,
To the soles of my feet mine offering be;
Come I with my name and my witnessing,
Come I with my contrite heart, confessing,
Come I unto thee, O Jesu my King –
O Jesu, do thou be my sheltering.

255   South Uist

The Soul-Shrine

God, give thy blest angels charge to surround
  Watching over this steading tonight,
A sacred, strong, steadfast band be they found
  To keep this soul-shrine from mischief-spite.

Safeguard thou, O God, this household tonight,
  Themselves, their means of life, their repute,
Free them from danger, from death, mischief-spite,
  From jealousy's and from hatred's fruit.

O grant thou to us, O God of our peace,
  Whate'er be our loss a thankful heart,
To obey thy laws here below nor cease,
  To enjoy thee when yon we depart.

165   Lochaber

Night Blessing

The dwelling, O God, by thee be blest,
And each one who here this night doth rest;
My dear ones, O God, bless thou and keep
In every place where they are asleep;

In the evening that doth fall tonight,
And in every single evening-light;
In the daylight that doth make today,
And in every single daylight-ray.

11

Smooring the Fire

The holy Three
For saving be,
To act as guard,
To aid and ward
The hearthstone fire,
The house entire,
The household all
As eve doth fall,
And night enthrall,
This evening light,
And o this night!
Each evening light,
Each single night,
So may it be,
O holy Three,
Amen to me.

506   *South Uist*

Resting Supplication

O God, preserve the house, the fire, the kine,
All those who here tonight in sleep recline.
Preserve myself, my love-fold children's band,
From attack keep us and from harm withstand;
Keep us this night from foes and hatred shun,
For the dear sake of Mary Mother's Son,
Here and each where tonight they resting dwell,
This evening's night and every night as well,
   This evening's night and every night as well.

166   Lochaber

Undressing Prayer

O thou great God, thy light grant to me,
O thou great God, thy grace may I see,
O thou great God, thy felicity,
And in thy health's well cleanse me pure-white.

O God, lift from me mine anguish sore,
O God, lift from me what I abhor,
O God, lift from me vanity's store,
And lighten my soul in thy love's light.

As I shed off my clothing at night,
Grant that I shed off my conflict-plight,
As vapours lift off the hill-crests white,
Lift thou my soul from the mist of death.

O Jesu Christ, O MacMary One,
O Jesu Christ, O thou Paschal Son,
My body shield in thy shield-cloak spun,
My soul made white in thy white grace-breath.

10

Bedside Prayer

O Jesu, the one who art sinless quite,
Thou humble King of the meek and the poor,
Who wast brought low and crucified so sore
By sentence of the evil men of spite,
Do thou defend and shield me for this night
From traitor-ways and Judas-dark-steal flight.

My soul on thine own arm, O Christ, to lie,
Thou art the King of the City of Heaven,
Thou it was, Jesu, who my soul didst buy,
For by thee was my life-sacrifice given.

Do thou protect me because of my woe,
For the sake of thy passion, wounds, thy blood,
Take me in safety tonight as I go
Climbing up near to the City of God.

106   *South Uist*

Night Sanctification

Father, bless me and my body keep,
    Father, bless me in my soul;
Father, bless me through this night of sleep
    In my body and my soul.

Father, bless me as I live my days,
    Father, bless me in my creed;
Father, bless me in my binding ways
    To my life and to my creed.

Father, sanctify to me my speech,
    Father, sanctify my heart;
Father, sanctify my portion each
    In my speech and in my heart.

257

Resting Blessing

In name of Rabbi Jesus of avail,
And of the Spirit of the balm so blest,
In the name of the Father of Israel,
      I lay me down to rest.

If any trick or evil threat there be,
Or secret that on me fate doth contrive,
May God encompass me and make me free,
      Mine enemy forth drive.

In the name of the Father richly dear,
And of the Spirit of the balm so blest,
In name of Rabbi Jesus who is near,
      I lay me down to rest.

O God, encompass me and give me aid,
From this hour till my death the hour invade.

510   South Uist

Repose

Of virtues thou Being,
        Shield me with thy might,
Thou Being decreeing
        And of the starlight.

This night be my compass,
        For body and soul,
This night be my compass,
        Each night compass whole.

Aright be my compass
        'Twixt earth and the sky,
Law-tight be my compass
        And for my blind eye;

That eye-caught belonging
        And that unread here;
That clear to my longing
        And what is unclear.

519

The Trinity at Night

With God will I lie down this night,
And God will be lying with me;
With Christ will I lie down this night,
And Christ will be lying with me;
With Spirit I lie down this night,
The Spirit will lie down with me;
God and Christ and the Spirit, Three,
Be they all down-lying with me.

517

Sleep-Dedication Prayer

O my God and O my Chief,
In morning light to thee I pray,
O my God and O my Chief,
Again this night to thee I pray.
I give unto thee belief,
I give my mind, my yea and nay,
I give unto thee my lief,
Body, and soul that lives for aye.

Mayest thou be unto me
Chieftain and master for my sway,
Mayest thou be unto me
Shepherd and guardian lest I stray,
Mayest thou be unto me
Herdsman and guide that I obey,
O Chief of chiefs, with me be,
God of the skies, Father for aye.

214

Quietude of Sleep

       O God of life, this night
O darken not to me thy light,
       O God of life, this night
Close not thy gladness to my sight,
       O God of life, this night
Thy door to me o shut not tight,
       O God of life, this night
Refuse not mercy to my plight,
       O God of life, this night
Quell unto me thy grieving slight,
       O God of life, this night
Crown thou to me thy joy's delight,
O crown to me thy joy's delight,
       O God of life, this night.

518   Kintail

Sleeping Prayer

My soul and my body this night I place
On thy sanctuary, O thou God of Grace,
On thy sanctuary, O Jesus Christ, here,
On thy sanctuary, Spirit true and clear,
    They who would stand to my cause, the Three,
          Nor coldly turn their backs on me.

Thou Father, righteous and kind one who art,
Thou Son, who o'er sin didst play victor's part,
Thou Holy Spirit of the mighty arm,
Give keeping to me this night from all harm;
    They who would my right uphold, the Three,
          This night and always keeping me.

509   South Uist

The Cross of Christ

Christ's cross 'twixt me and the folk of the hill
    That stealthily out or in do go,
The cross of Christ betwixt me and each ill,
    Each evil will, each misliking woe.

Be the angels of heaven shielding me,
    The heavenly angels for this night,
Be the angels of heaven shielding me
    Soul and body together aright.

The circle of Christ my compass around,
    From every spectre, from every bane,
And from every shame that comes to confound
    In darkness, and in power to give pain.

The circle of Christ my compass in might,
    My shielding from every harmful thing,
My keeping from each destruction this night
    Approaching me on destroying wing.

102   Barra

GOD, BLESS

The Homestead

O God, bless my homestead,
  Bless thou all in there.
O God, bless my kindred,
  Bless thou my life-share.

O God, bless my speaking,
  Bless thou what I say,
O God, bless my seeking,
  Bless thou all my way.

O God, sin decreasing,
  Increase thou belief.
O God, woe surceasing,
  Ward off from me grief.

God, from guilt be my shield,
  With joy be I filled.

O God, of my body
  Let naught harm my soul
When to great MacMary
  I enter in whole
In fellowship union
  Of his communion.

171

Family Blessing

Bless, O our God, the fire here laid,
As thou didst bless the Virgin Maid;
O God, the hearth and peats be blest,
As thou didst bless thy day of rest.

Bless, O our God, the household folk
According as Lord Jesus spoke;
Bless, O our God, the family,
As offered it should be to thee.

Bless, O our God, the house entire,
Bless, O our God, the warmth and fire,
Bless, O our God, the hearth alway;
Be thou thyself our strength and stay.

Bless us, O God Life-Being, well,
Blessing, O Christ of loving, tell,
Blessing, O Holy Spirit spell
With each and every one to dwell,
  With each and every one to dwell.

170   *South Uist*

House Blessing

God bless the house from ground to stay,
From beam to wall and all the way,
From head to post, from ridge to clay,
From balk to roof-tree let it lay,
From found to top and every day
God bless both fore and aft, I pray,
Nor from the house God's blessing stray,
    From top to toe the blessing go.

168   *North Uist*

For the Household

God, bless the world and all that in it dwell,
God, bless my partner, children dear as well,
God, bless the eye that stands set in my head,
And, God, the handling of my hand o bless;
What time I rise in morning's earliness,
What time I lie down late upon my bed,
  My rising bless in morning's earliness,
  And my late lying down upon my bed.

God, guard the household members and the hall,
God, consecrate the mother's children all,
God, all the flocks and young in safety keep;
Be after them and tend them from the fold,
What time the herds ascend the hill and wold,
What time I lie me down in gentle sleep,
  When slow the herds ascend the hill and wold,
  When tired I lie me down in peace to sleep.

161   *Lochaber*

The Prayer of Baptism

The little wave for thy form complete,
The little wave for thy voice so meet,
The little wave for thy speech so sweet.

The little wave for thy means requite,
The little wave for thy generous plight,
The little wave for thine appetite.

The little wave for thy wealth at hand,
The little wave for thy life in land,
The little wave for thy health to stand.

Nine waves of grace to thee may there be,
Saving waves of the Healer to thee.

The fill of hand for thy form complete,
The fill of hand for thy voice so meet,
The fill of hand for thy speech so sweet.

The fill of hand for thy mouth so small,
The fill of hand for thy fingers all,
The fill of hand to make strong and tall.

The fill of hand for the Father one,
The fill of hand for God's only Son,
The fill of hand for the Spirit done.

Nine fills of hand for thy grace to be,
In name of the Three-One Trinity.

45

The Mother's Farewell

The blessing of God, be it thine,
The blessing of Christ, be it thine,
The blessing of Spirit be thine,
On thy children be it to shine,
On thee and thy children to shine.

The peace of God, may it be thine,
The peace of Christ, may it be thine,
The peace of the Spirit be thine,
Thy whole span of life to refine,
All thy days and life to refine.

Shield of God in the pass be thine,
Aid of Christ in the gorge be thine,
Spirit-water in stream be thine,
Every going thou dost design,
A land or an ocean design.

The Father eternal's shield thine,
Upon his own lit altar-shrine;
The Father's shield always be thine,
Eternal from his altar-shrine
Lit up by gold taperflame-shine.

405

Grace of Love

Thine be the grace of love when in flower,
   Thine be the grace of humble floor,
Thine be the grace of a castled tower,
   Thine be the grace of palace door,
   Thine be the pride of homeland place
           And its grace.

The God of life to encompass thee,
Loving Christ encompass lovingly,
The Holy Ghost encompasser be
Cherishing, aid, enfolding to send
           To defend.

The Three be about thy head to stand,
   And the Three be about thy breast,
The Three about thy body at hand
   For each day, for each night of rest,
   The Trinity compassing strong
           Thy life long.

191

Peace between Neighbours

Peace between neighbours near,
Peace between kindred here,
Peace between lovers dear,
In love of the King of us all.

Peace man with man abide,
Peace man to wife allied,
Mother and bairns to guide,
And peace of the Christ above all.

Bless, O Christ, bless my face,
My face bless every face,
Christ, bless mine eye with grace,
Mine eye give a blessing to all.

316   Gairloch

The Peace of Everlasting

Peace of all felicity,
Peace of shining clarity,
Peace of joys consolatory.

Peace of souls in surety,
Peace of heav'n's futurity,
Peace of virgins' purity.

Peace of the enchanted bowers,
Peace of calm reposing hours,
Peace of everlasting, ours.

324

The Encompassing of the Three

The compassing of God be upon thee,
  God of the living encompassing.

The compassing of Christ be upon thee,
  The Christ of loving encompassing.

The compassing of Spirit be on thee,
  Holy Ghost laving encompassing.

The compassing of the Three be on thee,
  Encompassing Three preserving thee,
  Encompassing Three preserving thee.

121

The Clasping of God

May the Father everlasting
Himself take you, round you casting
His own gen'rous arm engrasping,
His own gen'rous hand enclasping.

118

God's Grace Distilling

The grace of God on you distil,
The grace of Christ bedewing fill,
The grace of Spirit flowing still
Each day and night upon you pour
Of this life's share for you in store;
  O day and night upon you pour
  Of this life's share for you in store.

187

The Trinity Pouring

Yours be the blessing of God and the Lord,
The perfect Spirit his blessing afford,
The Trinity's blessing on you outpoured
With gentle and gen'rous shedding abroad,
So gently gen'rously for you unstored.

47

The Eye of the Great God

May the great God's eye, beholding
God of glory's eye be seeing,
Eye of Virgin's Son be freeing,
Gentle Spirit's eye, enfolding,
Shepherd's aiding to thee showing
   In every time, in every clime,
   Each hour on thee outpouring be
In a gentle, gen'rous flowing.

352

The Three Rich and Generous

The eye of God with thee to dwell,
The foot of Christ to guide thee well,
The Spirit's pouring shower to swell
Thy rich and gen'rous fountain-well.

195

Good Wish

Eye that is good be good to thee,
Good of liking unto thee be,
   The good of my heart's desire.

Sons that are good to thee be born,
Daughters good to thee fair as dawn,
   The good of my sense's fire.

Thine the good of the good wide sea,
Thine the good of land fruitfully,
   Good of Prince of heav'nly quire.

196

Christ's Safe-Guarding

O the Christ's guarding that it may
Safe shield you ever and a day.

418

A Joyous Life

A joyous life I pray for thee,
Honour, estate and good repute,
No sigh from thy breast heaving be,
    From thine eye no tear of suit.

No hindrance on thy path to tread,
No shadow on thy face's shine,
Till in that mansion be thy bed,
    In the arms of Christ benign.

198

God's Blessing be Thine

God's blessing be thine,
And well may it spring,
The blessing divine
In Thine every thing.

197

Peace for this Life

The peace of God be unto you,
The peace of Jesus unto you,
The peace of Spirit unto you,
Be peace unto your children too,
Peace unto you, your children too,
Each day and night let there be peace
Till of this world your portion cease.

323

The Creator's Love

God the Father uncreate
      Above,
Your Creator Potentate
      In love,
Be with you in lovingness
      And bless.

199

The Kindly Lantern

The very self of the Mary Virgin's Son
   To you a kindly lantern may he be,
   Over your head a guiding, shining one
For the wide rough ocean of eternity.

433

By Mountain and Glen and Plain

The King to shield you in the glen,
The Christ to aid you on the ben,
Spirit to bathe you on the brae,
Hollow, or hill, or plain your way,
Be glen, or ben, or plain your way.

408

The Peace of God to You

Peace of God be unto you,
Peace of Christ be unto you,
Peace of Spirit be to you,
Peace be to your children too,
To your children and to you.

317